This book is presented to:

_____

From:

_____

Date:

_____

Jack Hayford Presents

the ACTS

BIBLE STORYBOOK

with Carol Wedeven

Illustrated by Dan Foote

Charisma
KIDS
A STRANG COMPANY

Jack Hayford Presents
the Acts Bible Storybook

Requests for information may be addressed to:

Charisma
KIDS

The children's book imprint of Strang Communications Company
600 Rinehart Rd., Lake Mary, FL 32746
www.charismakids.com

Children's Editor: Gwen Ellis
Copyeditor: Jevon Oakman Bolden
Design Director: Mark Poulalion
Designed by Joe De Leon

Library of Congress Cataloging-in-Publication Data

Hayford, Jack W.
  [Acts Bible storybook]
  Jack Hayford presents Acts Bible storybook / with Carol Wedeven ; illustrated by
Dan Foote.
      p. cm.
  ISBN 1-59185-211-0 (casebound)
  1. Bible stories, English--N.T. Acts. I. Title: Acts Bible storybook. II. Wedeven,
Carol, 1942- III. Foote, Dan. IV. Title.
BS2628.H39 2005
266.6'09505--dc22

                                    2004012767

05 06 07 08/ LP / 5 4 3 2 1
Printed in China

A WORD TO PEOPLE WHO CARE ABOUT KIDS

When CharismaKids wrote saying, "Pastor Jack, we would like you to do a book for children," my heart leaped inside me. Anna and I have four children, eleven grandchildren, and one great grandchild. Given our experience, I believe in the staying power of the material you sow into children's minds when they are young! *Truth made accessible and enjoyable will become truth remembered and applied later in life.*

Imagination is a gift from God, and it doesn't find any more vivid place of activation than in the heart and soul of a child! However, there are distinct limits to be honored when the Bible is the source of your basic story. Deciding how to exercise imagination that is honest with human experience; links up with the actual historical setting of the time; and, above all, stays faithful to the text of Scripture, calls for some serious thought. I believe that in this book we have exercised imagination and yet stayed true to both the Scripture and to the historical setting of the time.

Jack Hayford Presents the ACTS Bible Storybook is a tool that cultivates a child's healthy imagination and also builds barricades against the lying images that life in our world can press on children's minds.

Blessings upon you and upon the kids to whom you read these stories. The great thing to remember is that as God worked in power in the hearts of early believers, He is ready to do the same thing in our kids today!

—Jack Hayford

CHAPTER 1
Wait for the Promise
Acts 1

A child sees the risen Jesus and hears His command to wait for the promise of the Father.

The good things of God are worth waiting for!

Timothy poked at the brown thing in a small dish.

"It's a cocoon," his friend John had told him. "Something beautiful is growing inside. One day soon you will see what it is."

"When?" Timothy had asked.

"Watch and wait."

Timothy sighed. "Waiting takes forever," he said. "Boring."

It had not been boring with Jesus. Crowds would gather to hear Jesus speak. Sometimes Jesus hugged Timothy and the other children.

"Children are special," Jesus told them with a smile. He was the best grown-up friend Timothy had ever had.

Then yesterday a disciple had come to their house. He said, "The soldiers have killed Jesus."

"No!" Timothy said. "I don't want it to be true." But it was true. Timothy cried, and so did everyone else.

The next morning Timothy and his mother went to the garden where Jesus was buried. Timothy saw a giant stone covering the door of the grave. Mean-looking soldiers with shiny swords guarded the door. Timothy shivered when one soldier looked straight at him.

Timothy asked his mother, "What's going to happen?"

"God will help us," she said. "We can only pray and wait."

The next day Peter and John came running. "Good news!" they shouted. "Guess what happened. The grave is open, and Jesus is not inside!"

"And I saw Jesus—alive!" a woman said.

"Is it possible?" Timothy asked.

That evening, the disciples came to his house. When Timothy peeked into the room, he saw Someone there with the disciples. It looked like Jesus. Could it be? Yes! Jesus was alive and talking with His friends! Timothy laughed and cried all at once.

Jesus told them that God's power had made Him alive again. Then Jesus told them, "Wait for the gift my Father promised. In a few days you will be baptized with the Holy Spirit. You will receive power, and you will be my witnesses."

Wait? Timothy thought. *Wait again?*

Forty days later there was more news. "We were

talking to Jesus when He suddenly went up into heaven," Jesus' friends said. "Angels came and told us to wait because Jesus would come back some day!"

Timothy was watching the cocoon when something poked its head out. A wet, wobbly creature slowly wiggled to the edge of Timothy's bowl and waved its wings in the air to dry. It was a beautiful butterfly. It lifted into the air, circled Timothy's head, and glided away.

Just then Timothy heard a wind, but he couldn't feel it. The sound seemed to come from the room where Jesus' friends had been praying.

Timothy went to see. Whoooooooshhhhhh! The sound was all around him. It filled up every space inside him. Timothy looked around. Over every person's head flickered a little fire.

"The Holy Spirit has come," one disciple said.

Even though Timothy couldn't see Jesus, He seemed to be so close. Timothy praised the Lord with the others. "Lord Jesus," he said, "good things happen when I wait for You!"

CHAPTER 2
What Was That Sound?
Acts 2:1–41

A servant girl working in the upper room is among other believers who are touched by tongues of fire.

The Holy Spirit is for all believers—even kids!

Hannah wiped sweat from her face. If only a cool breeze would pass through the streets of Jerusalem. She waited for Zipporah to fill the water jar.

Both girls were servants, and their job today was to take water from the well to the believers who were praying.

Zipporah's family had moved to Jerusalem from far away. She spoke a different language than Hannah. They could not understand each other's words, so Hannah hummed and Zipporah hummed along, too. Then Hannah sang, "Wait, God's gift is coming. His gift is coming soon."

Ten days had passed since Jesus had gone back to

heaven. "Wait for God's gift," Jesus had said. Since then, many of Jesus' friends had been waiting and praying in the room upstairs.

It's hard to wait for something great, thought Hannah as she and Zipporah carried water jugs into the room.

Whooooooosh! A sound filled the house.

"What is it?" she cried. At that moment Hannah felt something strange and new. "God," she asked, "is this Your gift? Did the wind bring Your gift?"

Just then Timothy peeked into the room, and his mouth dropped open. Hannah turned to see what he was looking at. Flames of fire seemed to sit on every believer's head. It wasn't scary at all. The believers' eyes shone with joy as they spoke new languages.

Then Timothy pointed to Hannah's head! Hannah looked up and saw a flame over her head, too. *I see fire, but I don't feel it. I do feel something inside me, though— something joyful.*

"God's gift," Hannah told Zipporah

Zipporah grinned with joy.

Hannah said, "Thank You, God, for Your gift."

Zipporah clapped her hands and praised God. Hannah understood her. Zipporah spoke in Hannah's language.

And then, at that exact moment, Hannah began to speak words that sounded strange to her. But surprise! Zipporah could understand Hannah!

"God's gift!" they said together, each in her own language.

Late in the day, when everyone had gone home, Hannah waved goodbye to Zipporah. They still couldn't speak each other's language, but they knew they had shared a miracle. They knew that God had filled everyone with His Spirit.

The good news of Jesus was just beginning. The wind of the Holy Spirit would soon spread God's love all around the world. Best of all Hannah, Zipporah, Timothy, and all the children of the world would have a part in telling others the good news about God's love.

CHAPTER 3
The Fellowship of Believers
Acts 2:42–47
A brother and sister experience church life at the beginning when "all believers…had everything in common."

The body of Christ is His people.

Susanna and Mother kneaded barley dough into round flat cakes. Mother flicked drops of water on the stones. The water spit and spattered. "They're hot enough," she said, raking cinders away.

Susanna laid her cakes on the stones. In a few minutes, she turned the cakes with a stick. When the cakes were baked, Susanna put them into Sarah's basket. Soon the basket was full.

Most believers in the Jerusalem church didn't have much, so everyone shared what they had. Susanna and Aaron's family shared with a widow named Sarah. She was like a grandmother to them. Today they had come to Sarah's house. Susanna and Mother cooked in the courtyard while Aaron and

Father fixed a leak in the roof.

Bang! Bump!

Sarah grinned. "That's Levi, my neighbor's goat," she said.

Aaron looked down from the roof into the neighbor's courtyard. "Levi is bumping the wall."

Susanna put salt and oil into a copper pot filled with boiling water. Mother tossed in wild beans and onions picked from fields around Jerusalem. Sarah added herbs from her garden and lentils that Hannah had brought. Sarah's face beamed. "Being together is good," she said. "Making soup together makes joy." The vegetables and herbs cooked slowly. Mother stirred the soup.

Susanna watched Father and Aaron. They chopped straw and mixed it with mud. Splat! Again and again they laid mud over and around the leak. Then they beat it and rolled it flat.

Father wiped his hands. "Let it dry. Then we'll seal it."

Bang! Bump! Crash!

"That goat is going to break either his head or the wall," said Father.

Father and Aaron carried their tools down the ladder. They washed themselves in Sarah's washing bowl.

Susanna sniffed. "The soup smells good. It's ready."

"We're hungry," Aaron said.

Sarah hobbled over to her stool and sat down. She was ready to eat. The family sat around her on the ground.

When they finished eating, Sarah told them a story. The children had heard it before. But that was all

right because they liked hearing the story over and over again.

"Last year I went to the temple," Sarah said, "I saw rich people bringing piles of coins for the collection box. I felt bad. I only had two copper coins to give. It wasn't much of an offering. I decided to give my coins anyway.

"The rich people looked at my ragged clothes. They saw me put my two coins in the box. They sniffed and walked away. But I didn't care. I felt warm in my heart. A little voice inside me said, 'You are rich because your heart is right.'"

At the end of Sarah's story, she always said, "Give your best to Jesus. You will always have enough."

Susanna jumped up to clean the bowls. Aaron hopped up to help.

Bump! Bang! Now Levi was at Sarah's gate.

"Who's there?" Sarah called even though she knew it was that silly old goat. "Looks like Levi escaped again." She opened the gate, and Levi came strolling in. "Just a minute," Sarah said, "I'll get some mint. He likes it, and we can coax him home."

She grabbed some mint and held it up. Levi said, "Maaaa-a-a-a-a!"

"Come along, Levi," said Sarah, "Let's go home." Levi trotted along behind Sarah. The children went, too. Aaron tied Levi to a bush, and Susanna patted the goat's head as he munched on the mint.

"We got him home together," said Susanna.

"Yes, together is good, even if it is about a goat," said Aaron, and they all smiled.

CHAPTER 4

The Beautiful Gate
Acts 3:1–11

*The brother of the crippled beggar finds a new song
when his older brother is healed.*

There are many kinds of healing in Christ.

Pluck, pluck, strum. Luke played a sad, slow tune on his lute. Gabriel, his brother, couldn't walk, so Luke brought him to the temple every day. Gabriel sat near one of the marble pillars at the Beautiful Gate and begged for money. People dropped coins into his basket.

Luke prayed, "It would make me happy if Gabriel could walk. Please, God, heal Gabriel's legs."

Gabriel called out, "Praise the God of Abraham! Something for the poor?"

Two men stopped. They looked straight into Gabriel's eyes.

"Look at us!" one of them said. Gabriel looked up.

The man opened his empty hands. "I don't have

money for you," he said, "but I will give you what I have." Luke watched.

The man said, "In the name of Jesus Christ of Nazareth, get up and walk!"

Gabriel laughed. "My feet and ankle bones feel different," he said.

The man took Gabriel's hand and pulled him to his feet.

"You can stand!" Luke jumped up. "For the first time in your life, you can stand! Can you walk?"

Gabriel took one step, then two steps, and then twenty more.

"I can walk. I can run!" he ran in circles. "I can jump!" he shouted as he jumped high. "I can hop," he said as he hopped up and down.

"Yahoo!" Luke cried, leaping into the air! "God has answered my prayer!"

A crowd gathered. "What happened?" someone asked.

"The crippled man who begs at the gate can walk!" a man said.

"I saw it with my own eyes," said Luke. "But miracles come only from Jesus or one of His apostles."

Then the man said, "We are apostles of Jesus. I am Peter, and this is John. We did not make this man walk. God did it to bring glory to Jesus."

Luke was so happy he couldn't help laughing. "No more sad songs for me."

His fingers moved quickly over the lute's strings playing a tune that was bright and joyful. "Praise God, who blesses us!" he sang. Pluckity, pluckity, strummmmm.

CHAPTER 5
A Praise Meeting
Acts 4:1–31

*A servant girl hears Peter's sermon before the temple
rulers and follows him to a praise meeting.*

Wisdom comes from the Holy Spirit.

Portia hurried through the dark, narrow streets of Jerusalem with loaves of fresh bread from her family's bakery. Her first stop was at the temple. Portia was worried. Her friends Peter and John had been arrested by the temple leaders. They would be questioned this morning.

The Lord is my Shepherd. The words went over and over in her worried mind.

"I am with you," said the small voice inside her.

"I hear You, Lord," Portia said.

Outside the temple, Portia heard shouts. "Praise God! Gabriel is healed!"

But inside the temple, she heard an angry ruler shouting, "Punish the apostles!"

"Lord," she prayed, "keep my friends safe." She hurried inside to deliver the bread.

Soon temple guards marched Peter and John past her and into a meeting room. Gabriel was there, too.

Portia listened as angry rulers pointed to Gabriel. "Who helped you heal this man?" the leader asked.

Here comes trouble, Portia thought.

The small voice said, "I will give them wise words."

"Thank You, Holy Spirit," Portia whispered.

Peter's face glowed. He said, "Gabriel was healed by Jesus...whom you crucified...whom God made alive again."

The rulers frowned. Portia was frightened.

"Take these men out of the room," the chief ruler commanded. So the guards led Peter, John, and Gabriel away. Portia got busy arranging the bread. What would happen next?

"Such boldness!" the rulers said all talking at once.

"Where does a fisherman learn to speak like that?" one man said.

"What shall we do with these men?" said another.

"If we punish them, the people will riot," one man said.

Then the chief ruler yelled, "Quiet!" Everyone stopped talking. "We'll warn them this time," he said. The guards led Peter, John, and Gabriel back into the room.

The chief ruler stared at Peter and John. "Never, ever teach about Jesus again," he said.

The apostle's faces glowed. "God says to obey Him first. We can't stop talking about Jesus."

The rulers gave up. "Go, but don't ever teach about

Jesus again…or else!"

Or else what? Portia thought. She picked up her empty baskets and followed Peter and John.

Now Peter, John, Gabriel, and Portia hurried to the believers' meeting where James was already leading in praise.

Hurry before the rulers change their mind, Portia thought.

As soon as they got to Joseph's house, they went to the room where the believers were praying. They stood waiting and listening.

When James said, "Amen," Peter shouted, "Amen!" All the believers whirled around to look.

"Look! God has kept Peter and John safe!" someone cried. Everyone burst into singing, praising God for the great things He had done.

"Gabriel," James said, "tell us what happened to you."

Gabriel jumped up. "God healed my legs," he said.

Then Peter and John told how God had rescued them. "We will not stop teaching about Jesus. We will obey God first," they said. "We are not afraid."

"Today I saw prayers answered," Portia said, "and God's Spirit is changing me. I'm not afraid anymore."

"Thank You, God," James prayed. "Our brothers are safe. The rulers still fight *against* Jesus, but we will fight for Him."

Suddenly, Joseph's house shook. The Holy Spirit filled every one of them with great joy.

"Let's tell everybody!" Portia's face shone. "Praise God!" she said. "From now on I'll ask the Holy Spirit to help me stand up for Jesus just like Peter and John did."

CHAPTER 6
Rhoda Opens the Gate
Acts 12:1–17

Children experience glory and trouble with the other believers.

Courage comes from the Holy Spirit.

Rhoda and Aunt Mary were getting ready for a wonderful party called Passover. Passover was a time to remember how God had led his people out of Egypt long ago. Now it was a time for believers in *Yeshua ha Meshiach* (that means "Jesus the Messiah") to rejoice together.

Rhoda and Aunt Mary worked hard to get the house ready for the big day. Finally, it was here. Rhoda sang as she sliced the roasted lamb.

Aunt Mary took flat loaves of bread from the clay oven. She listened to Rhoda's song. Then she said, "Rhoda, I believe you are old enough to greet our guests."

"Really, Aunt Mary!" Rhoda was excited, because on such a day as this, answering the door and welcoming guests was an honor.

She began to practice what she would say. "Welcome beneath this roof tonight. Welcome in the name of the Lord God of Israel."

After a while the guests came. Rhoda greeted each of them. Soon the happy guests were eating, drinking, laughing, and singing. The whole house rang with a new Passover song the believers in Jesus had learned.

> *As long ago in Egypt, the power of God was shone.*
> *The Lamb was slain; the blood was placed on*
> *doorways of our homes.*
> *Our fathers all escaped their bonds as slaves in*
> *Egypt land,*
> *As Red Sea waters opened up through God's*
> *almighty hand.*

Then, everyone began to clap, and the dancers moved more rapidly as they all sang the chorus.

> *He's our God of great deliverance,*
> *Who provided us the saving Lamb.*
> *The Lamb of God, Yeshua, is our strong Deliverer,*
> *He's God's gift for our deliverance!*

The song ended with a great shout. Everyone was breathless and laughing.

Suddenly there was a sharp knock on the door. Aunt Mary said to Rhoda's big brother Samuel, "Go with Rhoda."

Moments later when Rhoda and Samuel opened the gate, Cleopas, a leader among Jerusalem's believers, rushed past them and into the room. He began speaking. "Dear friends," he said. "I have bad news. Herod's soldiers have put many believers in jail.

They have put Peter in the inner prison. And I am so sorry to report that they have killed James!"

Everyone gasped. James was the leader of the believers in Jerusalem. Rhoda was frightened.

People began to cry. Then Rhoda's father spoke. "My dear friends," he said, "We must pray. This feast day is a time to remember God's power. Long ago on Passover God's power set the Jews free and His power can free Peter today."

Rhoda prayed asking the Lord for strength and power.

Knock, knock!

Rhoda listened. *What was that?*

She tiptoed to the gate. She was shaking. Then in her heart she heard the Holy Spirit whisper, "Don't be afraid. I will help you."

She called out, "Who...who...who's there?"

"It's me...Peter."

It couldn't be, thought Rhoda. *Peter's in prison.* She called again, "Who?"

She heard a chuckle. "Rhoda. It's me, Peter. Let me in."

But Rhoda was so happy she forgot to open the gate. Instead she ran upstairs shouting, "It's Peter. Peter's at the gate!"

"It can't be," the believers said. "Maybe you dreamed it."

"No, it is Peter. Come see." They all hurried downstairs.

"Open the gate!" Peter said.

"Peter!" the believers said. "Praise God!" They opened the gate, and Peter came in. Rhoda locked the gate again.

"What happened?" Rhoda's father asked.

"Soldiers chained me in the jail," Peter told them. "While I was sleeping, a stranger touched me and said, 'Get up.' When I got up, my chains broke and fell to the floor. I thought I was dreaming. Then the stranger said, 'Get dressed.' So I did. I still didn't know what was happening.

"I followed the stranger right past two guards. When we came to the iron prison gate, it opened and then we were in the street. At that moment the stranger disappeared. Then I knew God's angel had saved me."

"It's a miracle," Rhoda squealed.

Everyone laughed and praised God again. Now Passover was even more wonderful because not only had God had freed his people from Egypt long ago, but he had freed Peter from prison today.

CHAPTER 7

The Sorcerer's Apprentice
Acts 8:1–25

Simon the Sorcerer's daughter becomes a believer.

The Holy Spirit is stronger than Satan.

Rachel felt her doll's forehead. She hung a necklace with a smooth stone around her doll's neck. "You are sick, Mayah," she said. "Maybe this magic stone will make you better." Rachel was playing with her doll in the marketplace near her father's magic shop. She was trying to heal her doll with magic because her father, Simon, had taught her magic could heal.

The marketplace was crowded with homeless people who had run away from Jerusalem. There, an awful man named Saul was trying to hurt or even kill those who believed in Jesus. So the believers had run away to Samaria where Rachel and her father lived.

Just then a man stood up and raised his hands. "I am Philip," he said. "I am the servant of Jesus of Nazareth; the One who was crucified and who then rose from the dead."

A blind beggar shouted, "I've heard Jesus healed blind people. If He's alive again, can He heal my eyes?"

That's impossible, thought Rachel.

Philip reached out and touched the man. He prayed, "Father God heal this man's blindness in the name of Jesus."

The man blinked and looked around. "I can see!" he cried. "Thank You! Thank You, God!"

Rachel's mouth dropped wide open. "What?" she cried. Then she thought, *I didn't see Philip's hands doing a trick, like Father does. Only God could do a real miracle like this!*

Rachel watched Philip touch more sick people as he prayed to God. And God healed them all.

"Father!" Rachel shouted, running to her father's magic shop. "Come, see."

Simon came and watched as Philip put his hands on a crippled man. "Hmmm," her father, Simon, mumbled. "I tried my magic on that old man last week, and I couldn't heal him. Unless I learn Philip's secrets, I won't be the greatest magician in Samaria anymore."

"Magic did not heal this man," Philip said. "Jesus, the Son of the one true God is alive, and He is here to heal and save you, too."

Rachel felt something happening inside her. It seemed as if dark was being crowded out by light. She listened some more.

"Philip," someone in the crowd called, "your God is the living God. He is the most powerful. Jesus is the greatest!"

For the next few days, Rachel and her father followed Philip around wherever he went. Rachel listened to learn more about Jesus. Simon watched to learn how Philip did his tricks.

Then one day Peter and John came to Samaria. They said, "We heard you now believe God's message. We have come to pray for you to receive the power of God's Holy Spirit."

Peter and John prayed for everyone, and they prayed for Rachel, too. When they prayed, something wonderful came into her like bubbling water into a cup. She felt bright and full. Her face shone, and she worshiped Jesus in a new way.

Then she heard her father ask Peter, "If I give you ten gold coins to buy this power, will you give it to me? Then I can do the things you do."

Peter spoke sharply to Simon. "There's something

very wrong with your heart and mind, Simon. You cannot buy God's gift. Your heart must be right. Repent. Stop the evil thinking that makes you want all the power for yourself. Ask God to forgive you. You're in a terrible trap."

All her life, Rachel had seen her father try to be the greatest. Now, Jesus—the truly greatest One—was here. Jesus wanted to free people from evil. But would her father ask?

Lord Jesus," Rachel prayed, "thank You for the Holy Spirit. Help me to follow You." She hugged her doll and said, "And Lord, help my father to truly love Jesus."

Then she untied the necklace with the smooth stone from her doll's neck. "We don't need this magic anymore, Mayah," she said. "We only need Jesus."

CHAPTER 8
Running With the Chariot
Acts 8:26–40

*A slave boy sees Philip appear and disappear,
and hears him explain God's Word.*

**God gives opportunities to witness
and lead people to Jesus.**

Rada ran fast next to his master's chariot. He and his master were on their way home from the Temple of the Living God in Jerusalem. Rada was the youngest servant in Kabede's caravan. His job was to run with other servants beside Kabede's chariot. It was an honor to go with Kabede on his special trip to worship God at the temple in Jerusalem.

As he ran, Rada thought, *I will worship the one true God. No more false gods.*

"Slow down," Kabede called to his driver. "The bumps make it difficult to read this book." The chariot slowed as it moved down the dusty road. At last Rada and the other servants could catch their breath.

"Listen to the Word," said a small voice inside Rada.

He had always wanted to know more about God, so he listened as his master read from the Book of Isaiah.

Kabede read aloud, "'He was led as a sheep to the slaughter. And as a lamb...silent before the shearers... he did not open his mouth.'" Kabede looked at Rada, "Young man, what do you think this means?"

"I don't know," said Rada.

"Who is this about?" Kabede asked another servant. That servant didn't know either.

Soon the caravan stopped to give the horses and runners a rest. As Rada rested, he looked across the desert and saw a man walking toward them.

"Master," Rada said. Kabede looked up as the man reached the chariot.

"Hello. Are you alone—way out here in the desert?" asked Kabede.

"Yes," said the man. "I came to help you."

Kabede was surprised. "What is your name?"

"I am Philip, a servant of the living God. What is yours?"

"I am Kabede, an officer in the court of Candace, queen of Ethiopia. I have been to Jerusalem to worship the one true God. Please come sit in my chariot."

Philip climbed up and sat beside Kabede. "I see you are reading the words of Isaiah," he said, smiling. "Do you understand them?"

Kabede shook his head. "How can I?" he said. "Who will teach me?"

"I will be happy to explain them," said Philip. "God has given us His Word. He will speak to your heart."

"Ride with me," Kabede begged.

The caravan began to move again. The horses trotted down the road. Rada ran, listened, and prayed. "Help us to understand Your Word," he whispered.

Philip told Kabede that long ago Isaiah talked about the Messiah who would die for everyone's sins. Philip told Kabede how Jesus had died and then came back to life. Jesus was the one who had fulfilled Isaiah's writings.

"Jesus?" asked Kabede. "The One called 'Messiah?' The One they say rose from the dead?"

"Yes," said Philip.

"Lord," Rada prayed, "how can we know this is true?

The small voice whispered inside Rada's heart, "Trust me."

Rada grinned. "I hear You, Lord," he said.

"Jesus is the Messiah," Philip told Kabede. "Men crucified Him, but God made Him alive again." Rada listened to every word. "If you believe in Jesus with all your heart," said Philip, "you can be baptized."

Kabede said, "I understand what you are saying. I believe that Jesus Christ is the Son of God."

So do I, Rada thought. *The story of Jesus is true.*

"Look!" Kabede said, pointing to a circle of trees, "Here's a pond. Can I be baptized?"

Philip said, "Because you believe, you can."

The driver stopped the chariot. Rada watched as Philip and Kabede got out and walked into the water. Philip said, "I baptize you, Kabede, in the name of the Father, the Son, and the Holy Spirit. In Jesus' name, receive His life and the power of His Spirit!" Philip

dipped Kabede into the water and lifted him up.

"Hallelujah!" Kabede shouted. The horses neighed.

"Hallelujah," whispered Rada.

Philip and Kabede came out of the water. Kabede climbed into the chariot and looked around for Philip.

"Where is Philip?" Kabede asked. He looked north, south, east, west, down the road, and over the desert. Philip was nowhere to be seen. He was gone.

The small voice whispered to Rada again, "I took Philip away to another place."

"Thank you, Lord," Rada said, "You brought Philip here just for us."

Soon the caravan moved quickly down the road toward Ethiopia. Rada was tired, but he bent his head, pumped his arms, and ran as fast as he could.

I can't wait to get home, he thought. *I have a great story to tell my family.*

CHAPTER 9

The Spirit Stops Saul
Acts 9:1–19

A servant sees Saul's transformation.

God wants us to know Him.

A ndrew piled sticks to build a fire at the campsite. The caravan was on its way from Jerusalem to Damascus. Next Andrew, Saul's young servant fed the horses and got them ready for the night.

Saul was a religious leader from Tarsus. Everyone in Jerusalem knew about him. Saul had never liked Christians. But now he had turned mean.

Today he was in a rage. He bellowed, "We'll crush those believer hypocrites tomorrow! We'll drag every Jesus believer back to Jerusalem in chains. Set up camp. Put the cart of chains where no one can steal them."

Chains were valuable and thieves liked to steal

them. Andrew put his bed roll under the chain cart. He would shout a warning if robbers sneaked into camp.

I'd be scared to death, Andrew thought, *but I can still yell.*

A voice whispered into his heart, "Don't be afraid. I am with you," it said.

"I hear You, Lord. Thank You," Andrew said, as he unrolled his blanket.

Andrew always did as he was told. *But what should I do when Saul attacks the Christians in Damascus?* he thought. *If Saul knew that I am a believer, he'd kill me. It's hard to obey God when I'm with a man like Saul.*

Early the next morning Saul yelled, "Let's go!"

As Andrew got the horses ready a voice within him said, "Don't be afraid of Saul. He's fighting against God. Pray for him."

The chain cart bumped along the rocky road. When the sun rose high in the sky, Andrew could see Damascus. *We'll be there soon,* he thought.

"Lord," he prayed, "warn the believers. Tell them to run."

Suddenly, like a shooting star, a dazzling white light, brighter than the sun, beamed from the sky. Saul, his men, and Andrew stood right in the middle of the bright light.

"God, help me!" Andrew said, covering his eyes. Then he slowly opened his fingers and peeked through the cracks. Saul had fallen to the ground.

He was talking quietly. He wasn't talking to Andrew or to any of his men. Everyone heard the voice, but

they didn't see anyone.

The voice asked, "Saul, Saul! Why do you persecute Me?"

Saul asked, "Who are You, Sir?"

"I am Jesus," the voice said. "Why do you persecute Me? Get up. Go to Damascus. Someone will tell you what to do."

Saul got up and looked around. "I can't see!" he cried, feeling the space near him. "I can't see anything." The men in the group were nervous. The bright light and the voice had frightened them.

Andrew looked around. When no one else went to help Saul, he did.

"Who are you?" Saul asked.

"It's me, Andrew. I'm the boy who takes care of the horses."

"Son, hold my hand. Where are the men?"

"Here, sir," Andrew said. "They don't know what to do," Andrew answered. "We all heard the voice, but we didn't see anyone."

"I saw a bright light," said Saul, "and now I'm blind."

"Sir, I will help you," Andrew said. Tell me what to do."

"Get two horses," said Saul. Andrew got two horses, he helped Saul mount his horse, and they rode toward Damascus.

At the Damascus gate, they got off their horses and Andrew led Saul to Straight Street to stay at the home of Judas.

For three days, Andrew brought food and water to Saul, but Saul would not eat or drink. His body was weak.

Andrew wondered what Saul was thinking. Then, the voice of the Holy Spirit said to Andrew's heart, "Saul is hungry for spiritual food."

When Andrew heard Saul praying, his heart beat faster. "Lord," he said, it's a miracle."

Saul prayed, "Lord, my eyes aren't a problem, but my heart is. Change my heart. I am ready to listen. I will do what you tell me to do."

On the third day someone knocked at the gate, and Judas and Andrew went to answer. The man at the gate said, "I am Ananias. The Holy Spirit of God told me to come to this house. Is Saul of Tarsus here?"

"Come in," Judas said. "Andrew, take this man to Saul." When they entered Saul's room, Saul reached out his hands, trying to touch Ananias.

"Saul," Ananias said, "the Lord Jesus told me what

He wants to do with you. I know He has spoken with you, too."

Saul listened like a peaceful child.

Ananias continued, "Jesus sent me to pray for you. Your eyes will see again, and you will be filled with the Holy Spirit." Then, Ananias laid his hands on Saul and prayed.

Almost immediately, flaky bits of skin fell from Saul's eyes. "Hallelujah! I can see!" he said, praising the Lord. His face glowed with a new smile, and his eyes twinkled. "Jesus, I believe!" he shouted.

Andrew brought Saul figs, olives, a loaf of bread, and some water. Saul ate and drank and began to grow strong again.

A few days later Saul told people what had happened. "Jesus is truly the Son of God!" he said.

Saul said to Andrew, "You have helped me, young man. Thank you. For me, this has been a time of great change."

Andrew grinned. "Yes, sir," he said. "And, sir, until now, I didn't like you very much. I was scared of you, but I needed the job to earn money."

Saul smiled and said, "Andrew, I didn't like myself either. Ever since I helped religious leaders kill a man named Stephen, I have not been able to forget the peaceful look on his face."

"Well, sir," said Andrew, "I'll always remember the angry man you used to be, and the nice man Jesus has made you. Jesus changed your heart and face from angry to peaceful."

CHAPTER 10

Tabitha Is Alive!

Acts 9:36–43

God raises Tabitha from the dead.

The Holy Spirit empowers us with miracles.

Stitch…stitch. Tabitha's fingers flew as they sewed. She was almost finished with a special embroidered coat for Mara. "I don't feel well enough to do any more today," Tabitha said. "I'll give it to Mara next Sabbath."

Mara was a little girl who lived near Tabitha and often came to visit. She liked to watch Tabitha sew. Tabitha sewed to earn money, and she sewed clothes for others just because she was kind.

On the next Sabbath Tabitha was ill. She could not meet with the believers, so she did not give the coat to Mara. In a few days, Tabitha died.

Everyone in Joppa was sad because they loved Tabitha.

"If only Peter were here," said one of the women who brought spices to prepare Tabitha's body for burial. "There are miracles when Peter prays."

"Peter is in Lydda," another said. "Perhaps someone can ask him to come." Two men went to find him.

They found Peter and told him, "Our friend Tabitha has died. Please come, and help us." Peter was sorry to hear that Tabitha had died. Then Peter hurried back with them.

At Tabitha's house, Peter went to the place where they had laid her body.

"Look, Peter, she made this coat for me," one of the widows said.

"She sewed for my children, too," said Mara's mother.

Mara's eyes filled with tears. She missed her friend.

Peter said, "Ladies, please leave the room." The ladies went downstairs, but Mara stood outside the door and peeked through a tiny hole. Peter prayed. Then he said, "Get up, Tabitha!"

Tabitha opened her eyes and saw Peter. She said, "Am I dead or alive? I saw Jesus."

Peter took her hand to help her stand. "You were dead," said Peter, "but now you are alive." He called the ladies.

Mara was the first to run into the room. She jumped into Tabitha's arms. "Oh, Tabitha!" she said. "I'm so glad you're alive! I love you!"

"I love you, too, Mara." Tabitha laughed and wrapped the beautiful new embroidered coat around the child. "My love gift to you," she said. Tabitha felt her face. "Praise God," she said, "I am alive!"

Mara hugged her coat around her. She and the believers shivered with excitement. They had seen the power of God. They ran out of the house and through the marketplace shouting the good news, "Tabitha is alive!"

Mara watched as crowds of people hurried to Tabitha's house. She came outside to greet them. "Peter is our special friend," she said, "but remember, Peter is not God. He did not heal me. God is the one who made me alive."

Then Peter told them all about the good news of God's Spirit. The people listened carefully. They wanted to know more. One by one they opened their hearts to Jesus, the Savior.

"Thank You, God," said Mara, "for my friend Tabitha, for my new coat, and for Your Spirit in my heart."

When most of the crowd had gone home, Mara found Tabitha.

"Thank you for my coat," she said. "It's beautiful!"

Mara looked at the embroidery on the coat. Tabitha pointed to a candle. "The candle," she said, "is to remind you that Jesus is the Light of life and that God our Father gave Jesus to you. Serve Him every day as long as you live."

Mara smiled and hugged her friend.

Tabitha said, "Jesus raised me up so I could get back to helping others." Once again she took her needle and set to work. Stitch, stitch, stitch. Stitchity, stitchity, stitch, stitch.

CHAPTER 11
A Storm on the Sea
Acts 27

*Paul goes through a storm at sea
and rescues a sailor's apprentice.*

The Holy Spirit is with me in trials.

Mark was the cabin boy on a very busy ship.
Every day he learned the lessons grown-up
sailors taught him. But today there would
be no lessons. A dangerous hurricane was coming.
Mark had never been in a storm at sea. He watched
as waves rose higher and higher. "Oh God," he
prayed, "who ever You are, please help me."

I wish our captain had listened to Paul, Mark thought.
*Paul said this trip would be dangerous. He told us not to
sail.*

The winds and rain whipped harder across the
deck, catching the sails and tossing the ship. Mark
and other sailors pulled in the sails. The storm was
driving the ship off course. Mark had heard about

ships blown off course during winter storms. He was afraid their ship would also be lost and destroyed and that everyone would be drowned.

"We're going to die!" the sailors cried. "May the gods help us."

The gods? Mark thought. *Their tiny, angry gods only make storms. I need a bigger and kinder God.*

Giant waves crashed on the deck, smashed barrels, and washed them into the sea. Mark watched the prisoner Paul. Paul was on his way to Rome to be put on trial. *Paul is different*, Mark thought. *He's not a criminal. Look at his face. He's not even afraid. I saw him praying to his God this morning. Whoever the true God is, I believe His Spirit helps Paul to be calm.*

The storm thundered. Waves pounded hard. Sheets of rain hid the black sky. There were no stars to show the way.

"We're lost! We're going to die!" Mark heard the sailors cry.

"God," he prayed, "please help us."

Then Mark heard a small voice inside him. "Don't be afraid," the voice said. "I am with you.

"Is this the one true God?" Mark asked. "Yes. It must be."

Sailors wrapped ropes around the ship to hold it together. They put out an anchor. Days passed. Almost everyone on the ship was seasick and terrified. Finally, the captain called everyone together.

"The ship is going to break apart!" the sailors cried. "Where are the gods when we need them?"

Paul stood up. "Men, God warned us not to sail, but you didn't listen. Now, please listen!" The crew and passengers listened. Mark listened, too.

"Hear me," Paul continued, "Don't be afraid. I belong to the living God. I serve the living God. Last night, a messenger angel of God brought me a message. He said that wild winds will break up our ship, but no one will drown. We must run the ship onto a beach."

Even though bigger waves lifted the ship higher than ever and the wind pounded it, Mark's heart felt peace. He believed Paul, and he knew the messenger angel's words were true.

The small voice inside said again, "I will help you."

Because Paul was not afraid, Mark could be brave, too.

Paul told everyone. "It's not time to leave the ship. Eat first. We will need strength to swim."

The sailors grumbled, but they ate anyway. Mark ate, too.

In the morning, Mark saw an island with a sandy beach. The sailors cut the anchors loose, put up the sail, and let the wind push the ship directly toward the island. The ship hit a hill of sand under the water and got stuck. The waves pounded the ship on every side.

Crack! Something jerked Mark off his feet. Crack! "The ship is splitting apart!" someone shouted. Sailors screamed and ran.

"Kill the prisoners! Don't let them escape," the guards cried.

"No!" shouted their leader. He didn't believe Paul was guilty. He knew Paul served the one true God. He ordered everyone to get in the water and to swim for the beach.

As Mark got ready to jump into the water, he prayed, "God, help me."

That same small voice said, "Find Paul." Mark saw Paul getting ready to jump off the ship. He reached out his hand to Paul. Paul grabbed it into his tight fist.

"Jump!" shouted the sailors. "We are lost!"

Mark shivered. "I'm afraid, Paul."

An inner voice answered, "Don't be afraid," and Paul said, "Come with me, son. The Lord will help both of us."

Paul hugged Mark close, and together they jumped into the cold water. Down, down they went. Then they swam upward. At last Paul pulled Mark up into the air.

Mark gulped and cried out, "Now what should I do?"

"Float on this board," Paul told him, pushing a board toward the boy.

Mark grabbed the broken board. Paul held onto Mark and the board. They kicked their feet and paddled toward shore.

Mark saw many shouting sailors splash through the waves. They cried and called to their gods. Some grabbed boards, too. At last they all dragged themselves onto the beach.

"It's a miracle," everyone said to Paul. "We are all alive! Not one of us has been lost. Your angel was right. Your God is powerful. It's a miracle. God saved us."

Mark raised his hands in praise. "Thank You, God," he shouted to the sky. "When I grow up, I want to have my own ship, and You, Lord, will be my Captain!"